99 Questions for Global Families
Quality Conversation Starters for Families Crossing Cultures

Copyright © 2018 by Jerry Jones
All rights reserved. This book or any portion thereof
may not be reproduced or used in any manner without
the express written permission of the publisher except
for the use of brief quotations in a book review.

For permission requests, write to the publisher, addressed
"Attention: Permissions," at connect@thecultureblend.com

Self Published
Qingdao, China
www.thecultureblend.com

"I never learn anything talking. I only learn things when I ask questions."

Lou Holtz

INTRODUCTION

Thanks for taking a look at this incredibly simple little book.

If your family is living cross-culturally then this was written especially for you.

You would think that a book full of questions would be all about finding some answers but that is not the case here.

Questions open the door to a whole new world of insight that is packed away just behind the eyeballs of the people we love. If you're like me though, you fall into the same rut over and over again.

"Hey. How ya' doin'? How was your day?

There is so much more available just for the asking.

I'm realizing that whether anyone in my family ever says it out loud, whether we consciously think about it or not, we are constantly processing the pieces of our global lives. The highs and lows, the adventure and the boredom, the never-ending paradox of living as foreigners with hearts in at least two places.

Here's the thing.

I WANT them to say it out loud and I want them to hear me do the same. I want to know what my family is thinking about our experience. I want insight into how my kids process our travels and our transitions and our bumbling mistakes as we figure out what normal looks like time and time again. I want them to know that I love this life . . . and I struggle with it too.

But (and this is a HUGE but)

NONE OF US is going to share that much information if the deepest question we ever ask is, "how was your day?"

So let's go deeper. One question a time.

Not big philosophical, life-changing questions but simple ones that peel back the layers and give us a glimpse into what is really going on inside.

Forget about the answers. The conversations are where the good stuff is.

The beauty of asking simple questions is that you discover so much more than just the answer.

I asked my daughter question number 42, "If you could choose five places to travel in the next year, where would they be?"

The answer changed three times during the discussion but this is what I discovered:

- She knows more about the world than I thought she did.
- She has thought about this before.
- She's more adventurous than I thought she was.
- Some of our choices match up.
- More than ever I want to go to those places with her.

That was ONE SINGLE question and I would bet cash that the answer would be different (for both of us) if I asked it again.

Answers don't matter.

The conversations are gold.

So start asking.

Pick a number from one to ninety-nine or skim the book, pick your favorites and dig in.

SOME GUIDELINES

- Value the conversation NOT the answer.

- Use the 8 accompanying question to discover more.

- Include your own questions. What are you curious to know?

- If a question doesn't apply, change it or move on. Don't stress about it.

- Listen intently. Share vulnerably. Repeat consistently.

Just for your reference:

PASSPORT COUNTRY = Passport of the person being asked.

HOST COUNTRY = The country you are living in.

Is it more complex than that for you? More than one passport? Hearts in more than two places? Don't let that stop you.

Adjust each question until it fits you perfectly.

You can check out the other books in the
99 Questions *series along with more great resources*
and insights into cross-cultural life at

www.thecultureblend.com

1
Where are you from?

> If you must give one answer, what would it be?
>
> Do you have more than one answer?
>
> How do you feel about this question?
>
> What are different ways to look at the question?
>
> What is difficult about this question and why?
>
> Has your answer ever changed?
>
> Do you think it will change in the future?
>
> How would your friends and family answer?

2

Would you like to live internationally 20 years from now?

Kids: When you grow up?

Parents: Do you want your kids to live abroad?

What would the challenges be?

What would the benefits be?

Do you think you would stay in one spot?

Where would you like to live?

Where would you NOT like to live?

Would you want to live in your passport country?

3
What is the best airport?

> What is your favorite airport?
>
> What makes it the best?
>
> What is your favorite airport restaurant?
>
> What makes an airport great?
>
> What do you not like at an airport?
>
> What is your least favorite airport?
>
> How many airports have you been to?
>
> What is your favorite airline?

4

How is technology different in your passport country and your host country?

What is available in one and not the other?

What is better in one than the other?

What could they learn from each other?

Which technologies are you most thankful for?

How would your life be different without tech?

Which tech would you give up for a week?

What are the negatives of great technology?

How has tech (here & there) changed in 5 years?

5

Of all your family and friends, who would be the funnest to travel with internationally?

Who would be the most fun on a trip?

Why would they be so fun?

Where would you like to go with them?

Do you think that will ever happen?

Why or why not?

How would they respond to different people?

How would they respond to different food?

What might be hard about traveling with them?

6

Of all your family and friends, who would be the most difficult to travel with internationally?

> Who would be the most difficult on a trip?
>
> Why would they be so difficult?
>
> How would they respond to airports?
>
> How would they respond to different foods?
>
> How would they respond to different people?
>
> How would you respond to them?
>
> Who in your family would handle them well?
>
> Who in your family would not handle them well?

7

What food do you love the most in your host country that you cannot get in your passport country?

What is your favorite host country food?

Why is it so good?

Have you ever seen it in your passport country?

Can you make it in your home?

Do you know if it is available in other countries?

Would people like it in your passport country?

How would you describe it to people?

Who do you know that would like it? Hate it?

8

What food do you love the most in your passport country that you cannot get in your host country?

What food do you love from your passport country?

Why is it so good?

Have you ever seen it in your host country?

Can you make it in your home?

Do you know if it is available in other countries?

Would people like it in your host country?

How would you describe it to your host country?

Who do you know that would like it? Hate it?

9

What is the best way to travel?

> What is your favorite form of travel?
> Airplane? Train? Car? Motorcycle?
> Bicycle? Walking?
> Why do you prefer it?
> What are the benefits of each?
> What are the challenges of each?
> What makes travel great?
> What makes travel hard?

10

If you could change one thing about your passport country, what would it be?

What would you change?

What would you do to make it better?

How would that impact the country?

How could it impact the world?

How would it impact your friends and family?

Would there be any bad side to it?

Who would be upset about it?

Do you think the change will actually happen?

11

If you could change one thing about your host country, what would it be?

What would you change?

What would you do to make it better?

How would that impact the country?

How could it impact the world?

How would it impact your friends and family?

Would there be any bad side to it?

Who would be upset about it?

Do you think the change will actually happen?

12

What places in the world would you NOT want to travel?

What places would you least like to travel?

Why do you not want to travel there?

What do you know about those places?

How did you learn about those places?

Which places would be the most dangerous?

Which places would be the most boring?

What would it take to change your mind?

Who do you think WOULD like to travel there?

13

How many capitals can you name?

How many national capitals can you name?

How many provincial/state/regional capitals?

Which capitals have you traveled to?

Which capitals would you most like to travel?

How many former capitals can you name?

Which capital is your favorite?

Which capital is your least favorite?

What's a story about a capital that you know?

14

What is the best thing about flying?

What do you like about flying?

Do you like the food?

Do you like turbulence?

Do you like to talk to new people on the plane?

Do you like watching movies on the plane?

What do you think of airplane restrooms?

What is a funny airplane story?

What are the best seats (that you have sat in)?

15

How many countries start with the letter "M"?

How many "M" countries can you name?

"G"?

"L"?

"S"?

How many countries start with North or South?

How many countries start with East or West?

How many countries have changed names?

How many countries start with "United"?

16

Who do you know from different continents?

Who do you know from Africa?

Who do you know from Asia?

Who do you know from Europe?

Who do you know from North America?

Who do you know from Oceana?

Who do you know from South America?

Do you know anyone with dual citizenship?

Would you ever travel to Antarctica?

17

How would your life be different if you lived in a different continent?

How would life be different if you moved to Africa?

Asia?

Europe?

North America?

Oceana?

South America?

Which continent would you most like to move to?

Which continent would you least like to move to?

18

What are five things that your host country does better than your passport country?

What does your host country do better?

Better foods?

Better laws?

Better arts, music, dance?

Better manners?

Why do you think it is better?

Who would agree with you?

Who would disagree with you?

19

What are five things that your passport country does better than your host country?

> What does your passport country do better?
>
> Better foods?
>
> Better laws?
>
> Better arts, music, dance?
>
> Better manners?
>
> Why do you think it is better?
>
> Who would agree with you?
>
> Who would disagree with you?

20

What is the best time of year?

> What is your favorite time of the year?
> What makes it the best time of the year?
> What is your favorite month?
> How would it be different if you moved?
> What events do you look forward to every year?
> Is there a time that gives you mixed emotions?
> What is the worst time of year?
> How has all of this changed over time?

21

What about your family never changes?

> What about your family is always the same?
>
> What would be the same wherever you live?
>
> What routines do you have?
>
> What are your "family foods"?
>
> What things are in your home that will always be?
>
> What would you take with you if you moved?
>
> What pictures have always been in your home?
>
> What are your family games?

22

What are your favorite special days/holidays/ celebrations?

What are your favorite special days?

Which ones from your host culture do you like?

Passport culture?

Do you have celebrations from other cultures?

Can you sing a song from a special day?

Can you sing one in a different language?

What is your favorite special day tradition?

What traditions do you think are strange?

23

What would a movie about your family be like?

What would your family movie be like?

What genre would it be (comedy, drama etc.)?

What would the main themes be?

Where would it be set?

What stories would be the funniest?

What stories would be the most exciting?

What actors/actresses would play each of you?

Who would want to see it?

24

What are the most memorable trips you have ever taken?

What family trips are memorable?

Why are they so memorable?

What are some funny stories from the trips?

Did you have challenges?

What people were memorable?

Would you go there again?

What trips were not so memorable?

How can you make your next trip memorable?

25

Who from your passport country do you think would be great at living in your host country?

Who would do well in your host country?

Who would be the most fun?

Who would love the food the most?

Who would do well adjusting?

Who would be great in your community?

Who would be helpful to other people?

Do you think they would ever consider moving?

Why or why not?

26

Who from your host country do you think would be great at living in your passport country?

Who would do well in your passport country?

Who would be the most fun?

Who would love the food the most?

Who would do well adjusting?

What would they think of life there?

What kind of work would they do?

Do you think they would ever consider moving?

Why or why not?

27

Who from your passport country could never live in your host country?

Who would not do well in your host country?

How would they react to the life?

What do you think would be frustrating for them?

What might they do that is embarrassing?

What would they think about the food?

What would they think about the people?

What would they like?

Would they ever consider living there?

28

Who from your host country could never live in your passport country?

Who would not do well in your passport country?

How would they react to the life?

What do you think would be frustrating for them?

What might they do that is embarrassing?

What would they think about the food?

What would they think about the people?

What would they like?

Would they ever consider living there?

29

Who in your family loves to travel the most?

Who, in your family really loves to travel?

What do they love about it?

How do they prefer to travel?

Are they fun or serious when they travel?

Do they like to travel together or alone?

What travel habits do they have?

Who likes to travel the least?

What do they not like about it?

30

How does your family travel?

As a family what are you like when you travel?

Who makes the plans?

Who does the packing?

What are your travel traditions?

How do you travel best (plane, car, train etc.)?

What are some favorite travel memories?

What's the worst part about traveling as a family?

How long is too long for a trip?

31

Who is the most "adventurous" eater in your family?

Who will eat just about anything?

What have they eaten that seems "adventurous"?

What is the "strangest" thing they have eaten?

What is the worst tasting thing they have eaten?

What is a story about "adventurous" eating?

What would they eat that others would not?

What would they not eat?

Who is the least "adventurous"?

32

Who in your family likes to meet new people the most?

Who enjoys meeting new people?

What do they like about meeting people?

Where do they meet people?

How do they start conversations?

How often do they make new friends?

Who likes meeting new people the least?

Who is the most/least comfortable in a crowd?

Who enjoys being alone the most?

33

How many African countries can you name?

> How many nations in Africa can you name?
>
> How many in total do you think there are?
>
> Which ones are completely landlocked?
>
> Which ones are coastal?
>
> Who do you know from those countries?
>
> What do you NOT know about Africa?
>
> What about Asia? Europe? Oceana?
>
> North America? South America?

34

If you had to change your citizenship, what country would you choose?

Where would you be a citizen if you had to change?

Why would you choose that country?

What would be different?

What would be the same?

What advantages would you have?

What disadvantages would you have?

Where, in that country, would you want to live?

Would you ever choose to change your citizenship?

35

How are elderly people different in your host and passport countries?

How are older people different in the two places?

What do they do for fun?

What do they do for exercise?

How do they treat or talk to children?

What do they do when they retire?

What is different between men and women?

What do they think of younger generations?

What is different about their life experiences?

36

How are children different in your host and passport countries?

> How are children different in the two places?
>
> What is different about how they have fun?
>
> What is different about their routines?
>
> How are their homes different?
>
> What is different about their families?
>
> What is different about how they are disciplined?
>
> How are they the same?
>
> What could they learn from each other?

37

How is education different in your host and passport countries?

What is different about education?

What is different about educational style?

What is different about educational philosophy?

What is different about schools?

What is different about grading systems?

What are the strengths of each?

What are the weaknesses of each?

How does education vary in each place?

38

How is safety different in your host and passport countries?

What are some safety differences?

How do people view safety differently?

What are some different rules and regulations?

What are some different practices?

What is different about crossing the road?

What is different about food safety?

What are the strengths of each?

What are the weaknesses of each?

39

Are you an introvert or an extrovert?

What are your personality types?

Who is the most extroverted in the family?

Who is the most introverted?

How do you like to spend time with friends?

Who likes to get the most attention?

Who does not like to draw attention?

Who likes to be alone the most?

How do you complement each other?

40

What would you tell someone who has never flown on an airplane before?

> What advice would you give a new flyer?
> Who do you know who has never flown?
> How should they prepare for a flight?
> What should they take on the plane?
> What should they NOT take on the plane?
> What would you tell them about checking in?
> What would you tell them about security?
> What about taking off and landing?

41

If you had to stay in one city/town/place for ten years, where would it be?

Where would you live if you could not leave?

Why would you choose that place?

What are some important factors?

What would be the best part about being there?

What would be the hardest part?

What would be scary about living there?

Does staying in one place sound good to you?

Why or why not?

42

If you could choose five places to travel in the next year, where would they be?

Where would you go this year if you could?

How did you choose those places?

Which is the one you would most want to go to?

How long would you stay at each place?

Who would you take with you?

What places or things would you see?

Which one would be at the bottom of the list?

What order would you travel in?

43

What are some drinks from your host country that you can't get in your passport country?

What are your favorite host country drinks?

Why do you like them?

What is different about the way people drink?

Would your passport country friends like them?

Would any of them seem strange there?

What are your least favorite host country drinks?

Why don't you like them?

What drinks are the same?

44

What are some drinks from your passport country that you can't get in your host country?

What are your favorite passport country drinks?

Why do you like them?

What is different about the way people drink?

Would your host country friends like them?

Would any of them seem strange?

What are your least favorite passport country drinks?

Why don't you like them?

What drinks are the same?

45

When you think of people that you miss, what stories do you remember?

Who do you miss from your passport country?

What are your favorite memories of them?

What is a funny story about them?

What did you do last time you were with them?

What is your earliest memory of them?

How could you let them know you miss them?

What would it be like if they came to visit you?

Do you think that will happen?

46

What is the worst smell you have ever smelled?

What was the worst smell you ever smelled?

What words would you use to describe it?

Where were you at the time?

Was it only once or have you smelled it again?

How did you react when you smelled it?

How did other people react?

Do you know what the source was?

What smells remind you of different places?

47

What does your passport country smell like?

What are some of your passport country smells?

Which smells come to mind?

What are the best smells?

What are the worst smells?

What smells remind you of family there?

What smells remind you of friends there?

What smells remind you of food there?

What smells remind you of specific places?

48

What does your host country smell like?

> What are some your host country smells?
>
> Which smells come to mind?
>
> What are the best smells?
>
> What are the worst smells?
>
> What smells remind you of people there?
>
> What smells remind you of experiences there?
>
> What smells remind you of food there?
>
> What smells remind you of specific places?

49

How is eating different in your host and passport countries?

What are the main differences in eating?

How is meal time different?

How are restaurants different?

How is the food different?

How do food prices compare?

How are table manners different?

How is meal preparation different?

How are utensils different?

50

How is driving different in your host and passport countries?

What is different about the way people drive?

How is traffic different?

What is different about vehicles?

What laws are different?

What is different about the speed people drive?

What are safety differences?

What are the benefits of each?

What are the challenges of each?

51

How many languages can you speak (even a little)?

> How many languages can you say at least 3 words?
>
> What words are they?
>
> Who can speak the most?
>
> How many can you count to ten in?
>
> How many can you sing songs in?
>
> Where/who did you learn from?
>
> Who do you know that speaks those languages?
>
> Who do you know that speaks the most languages?

52

How many languages can your friends speak?

How many languages do your friends speak?

Where are they from?

How many speak more than one language?

Who speaks the most?

Which language would you most like to learn?

Which language do you think would be hard?

Which language would be the easiest?

Which friend would you like to travel with?

53

How many countries do you know people from?

How many countries do you know people from?

Where are your closest friends from ?

Which countries do you have the most friends?

Which continent is most represented?

What is the coldest country you know someone from?

What is the warmest?

What is the closest to the equator?

Which of their countries would you like to visit?

54

If you could learn one language instantly, what would it be?

What language do you wish you could speak?

Why would you choose that one?

What could you do if you spoke it?

Where would you go?

Do you know people who speak it?

How much can you speak now?

Would it be hard or easy to learn?

Do you think you will ever learn it?

55

What would be different if you lived where you live now, 20 years ago?

What has changed in the last twenty years?

How would your life be different?

How have people changed?

What would not be available?

What about 50 years?

100 years?

How would you be viewed differently?

How has technology changed the culture?

56

How would you finish this sentence? "My HOST country is _____"

What words describe your host country?

What is your first, quick answer?

Does it change if you think about it?

What influences your answer?

Is your sentence positive?

Is your sentence negative?

How would you change it to be the other?

How would other people see it differently?

57

How would you finish this sentence? "My PASSPORT country is _____"

What words describe your passport country?

What is your first, quick answer?

Does it change if you think about it?

What influences your answer?

Is your sentence positive?

Is your sentence negative?

How would you change it to be the other?

How would other people see it differently?

58

What are the oldest things you've ever seen?

What have you seen that is really old?

What is the oldest building or structure?

What is the oldest city?

What is the oldest tree?

Who is the oldest person you've ever met?

What is the oldest car/vehicle?

What is the oldest thing you own?

Do old things interest you? Why or why not?

59

How is exercise different in your host and passport countries?

What is different about how people exercise?

What exercises do each do?

What is the focus (health, strength, looks etc.)?

When do people exercise?

Do people pay to exercise?

Is it expensive?

Where are people generally healthier?

Is there a culture of health and exercise?

60

Where would you travel tonight if you had a private jet?

Where in the world would you like to go?

Where have you always wanted to visit?

What's the first thing you would do there?

How long would you stay?

Who would you take with you?

What would you eat there?

Where would you go after that?

And after that?

61

How is going to the doctor different in your host and your passport countries?

What is different about going to the doctor?

What is different about the building?

What is different about the nurse/helpers?

What is different about the doctor?

What is the price difference?

What is different about the wait time?

Which is nicer/cleaner?

Which do you prefer?

62

How is shopping different in your host and your passport countries?

What is different about shopping?

For food?

For clothes?

For cleaning supplies and household items?

How are prices different?

How are stores different?

How are helpers/workers different?

How is bargaining different?

63

Who do you know that has never traveled internationally?

Who has never left their country?

Friends?

Family?

Why do you think they haven't?

Do you think they would like international travel?

Why or why not?

Would you like to stay in one country only?

Why or why not?

64

What does your host country's flag mean?

What does your host country's flag represent?

What are the meaning of the colors?

What are the meaning of the symbols?

What is the history of the flag?

Have their been other flags?

Who displays the flag (people, places, etc.)?

What traditions are connected to the flag?

What emotions are connected to the flag?

65

What does your passport country's flag mean?

What does your passport country's flag represent?

What is the meaning of the colors?

What is the meaning of the symbols?

What is the history of the flag?

Have their been other flags?

Who displays the flag (people, places, etc.)?

What traditions are connected to the flag?

What emotions are connected to the flag?

66

How would you define home?

What is your definition of home?

Is home a place, people or something else?

How do you know when you are home?

Can you have more than one home?

Is home hard to define?

Why or why not?

Do you consider a country home?

Which one?

67

How are games different in your host and passport countries?

> How are games different?
>
> What do people do for fun?
>
> How are sporting events different?
>
> How are children's games different?
>
> Who plays games?
>
> Are there different card games?
>
> What games are most popular?
>
> What are your favorite games from each?

68

What stereotypes does your host country have of your passport country?

What do people think of your passport country?

What are the things that they assume to be true?

What are the most asked questions?

What are the positive stereotypes?

What are the negative stereotypes?

What are they most right about?

What are they most wrong about?

How do you think they can learn more?

69

What stereotypes does your passport country have of your host country?

What do people think of your host country?

What are the things that they assume to be true?

What are the most asked questions?

What are the positive stereotypes?

What are the negative stereotypes?

What are they most right about?

What are they most wrong about?

How do you think they can learn more?

70

Who has taught you the most about your host culture?

Who has been your best host culture teacher?
What is an example of what they've taught you?
What makes them a great teacher?
What important things have they taught you?
Who else has taught you?
Who would you ask if you had a question?
What questions do you still have?
How could you show appreciation?

71

Who has taught you the most about your passport culture

Who has taught you about your passport culture?

What's an example of what they've taught you?

What makes them a great teacher?

What's important things have they taught you?

Who else has taught you?

Who would you ask if you had a question?

What questions do you still have?

How could you show appreciation?

72

What makes a great family adventure?

> What do we love to do as a family?
>
> What are the pieces of an adventure?
>
> Who is the most adventurous?
>
> What are some of our favorite adventures?
>
> What was our last adventure?
>
> What does "adventure" mean for our family?
>
> How is our "adventure" different from others?
>
> What should our next adventure be?

73

What have you learned about other countries because you live abroad?

What have you learned about the world?

What have your friends taught you?

What have you learned as you travel?

What have you learned about people?

What have you learned about government?

What have you learned about food?

Where have you learned the most?

What would you like to learn next?

74

What language do you think would be the hardest to learn?

Which language would be the hardest?

Why do you think it would be so hard?

What makes a language hard to learn?

Do you know anyone who speaks that language?

How long do you think it would take to learn?

What language would be the easiest to learn?

Why would it be so easy?

What other languages would be hard to learn?

75

Would you rather go to the ocean or mountains?

Would you rather go to the beach or a mountain?

Go to a new country or stay close?

Go on a cruise or stay in a resort?

Go touring with a guide or explore on your own?

Stay in a hotel or go camping?

Go on a road trip or fly somewhere?

Eat a fancy meal or street food?

Relax or go, go, go?

76

How would you finish this sentence? "I don't understand why my host country..."

What confuses you about your host country?

Why is it confusing?

How long has it confused you?

Do you think most people are confused as well?

Who could you ask about it?

Are there other things that confuse you?

How would other people finish the sentence?

What do you think confuses them about you?

77

How would you finish this sentence? "I don't understand why my passport country..."

What confuses you about your passport country?

Why is it confusing?

How long has it confused you?

Do you think most people are confused as well?

Who could you ask about it?

Are there other things that confuse you?

How would other people finish the sentence?

What is confusing about your host to them?

78

How many countries have you been to (separately or together)?

What is your total country "been there" number?

Which countries have you been to?

Who has been to the most?

Who has been to the least?

Can we identify all of their flags?

Do airports count?

What is your goal number?

What should the next new country be?

79

How many cities of more than 1 million people have you been to (separately or together)?

What is your total big city "been there" number?

Which big cities have you been to?

Who has been to the most?

Who has been to the least?

Which are your favorites?

Do airports count?

What cities would we like to go to?

What should the next new big city be?

80

Who do you wish you could meet?

If you could meet anyone who would it be?

Someone famous?

Actor or actress?

Famous sports star?

World leader?

What would you ask them?

Where would you meet them?

Why did you choose them?

81

How many islands can you name?

How many islands do you know?

Could you find them on a map?

What's the largest island you know?

What is the closest island to you?

Which ones would you like to visit?

Would you like to live on an island?

What would be most enjoyable?

What would be most difficult?

82

What would be the best climate to live in?

What climate do you prefer?
Would you like to live where it is hot?
Would you like to live where it is cold?
Is it important to have changing seasons?
What place has the best climate?
Do you know anyone who lives there?
What is too hot?
What is too cold?

83

Which two friends or family members would it be awkward if they met?

Who do you know that should never meet?

What would be awkward about it?

What do you think would happen?

What would be said?

How would you react?

Do you think they could be friends?

What are the chances that they could ever meet?

What friends would you love to have meet?

84

What law would you change in your passport country?

What law should be changed?
Why should it be changed?
How would you make it different?
Who would be the most impacted?
Would there be negative effects?
Do you think it will ever actually change?
How has it changed in the past?
What countries do it better?

85

What law would you change in your host country?

What law should be changed?

Why should it be changed?

How would you make it different?

Who would be the most impacted?

Would there be negative effects?

Do you think it will ever actually change?

How has it changed in the past?

What countries do it better?

86

If you could only eat food from one country/region, who would you choose?

What kind of ethnic food do you like the best?

What dishes are your favorite?

What is so good about it?

What restaurant/person makes it the best?

What is your least favorite ethnic food?

What do you not like about it?

What other food would you miss the most?

What food would you like to try that you haven't?

87

What are some pictures that you want to have but don't have yet?

What are some pictures you should take?
What pictures do you want to show someday?
What nearby places would you like a picture of?
What people are you missing pictures of?
What people would you like more/better pics of?
What pictures from your passport country?
What travel pictures?
What selfies?

88

What is the flavor of your family?

What is unique about your family?

What is special about your family?

What is weird about your family?

What do you love most about your family?

What adjectives describe your family?

What makes your family fun?

What are your routines?

What makes your different than other families?

89

Who are the heroes in your passport country?

Who is considered a hero?

What are they known for?

What is their story?

How are they recognized/revered?

What values do they represent?

Do/did they have enemies?

Do you agree that they are a hero?

How have heroes changed over time?

90

Who are the heroes in your host country?

> Who is considered a hero?
>
> What are they known for?
>
> What is their story?
>
> How are they recognized/revered?
>
> What values do they represent?
>
> Do/did they have enemies?
>
> Do you agree that they are a hero?
>
> How have heroes changed over time?

91

What ten landmarks would you like to see in the world? (like the Eiffel Tower or the Pyramids)

What world landmarks would you like to see?

Where are they located?

What makes them interesting to you?

What do you know about their history?

Do you know anyone who has seen them?

Who would you take with you?

Do you think you will ever go?

What famous landmarks do not interest you?

92

What are your family traditions?

What traditions does your family have?

Holiday traditions?

Birthday traditions?

Other special day traditions?

Where did your traditions come from?

What are your favorite traditions?

What are your oldest traditions?

What new traditions should you start?

93

What are your family values?

What is most important to your family?

What ideas?

What beliefs?

What actions, characteristics, manners etc.?

How do your values reflect your passport country?

How do your values reflect your host country?

How are your values different from others?

What are your most important values?

94

What skills do you want to develop over the next five years?

What new skill would you like to learn?

What current skill would you like to get better at?

Why?

How difficult would it be?

What would it take to learn/get better?

Who do you know that does it well?

Do you think you will do it?

What is the next step?

95

What subject or topic would you most like to learn about?

> What topics interest you?
>
> Why do they interest you?
>
> How could you learn about them?
>
> Who are the experts on those topics?
>
> Do you think you will actually learn about it?
>
> What would prevent you?
>
> What is the next step?
>
> When will you start?

96

What would you miss the most (besides people) if you moved away?

> What things would you miss if you moved?
>
> What places would you miss?
>
> What food would you miss?
>
> What traditions would you miss?
>
> What activities would you miss?
>
> How would you keep them a part of your life?
>
> What would you take with you?
>
> What could you not take with you?

97

Who would you miss the most if you moved away?

> What people would you miss if you moved?
>
> What kids would you miss?
>
> What adults would you miss?
>
> Who has helped/impacted you the most?
>
> How have they helped/impacted you?
>
> How would you stay in touch with them?
>
> How would you tell them you will miss them?
>
> Which friends do you think will be lifelong?

98

What will change in the next 10 years?

What will your lives be like in 10 years?

Where will you live?

What will you be doing?

What will be the biggest differences?

What scares you about the future?

What excites you about the future?

Who will change the most in 10 years?

Who will change the least?

99

What will you take with you no matter where you go?

> What will go with you wherever you go?
> What physical things would you take?
> What is the biggest thing you would take?
> What is the smallest thing you would take?
> What ideas would you take with you?
> What traditions would you take with you
> What values would you take with you?
> What memories would you take with you?

Note

When you have asked ALL 99 Questions to
ALL of your global friends . . . start over.
See what you learn the second time.

Never stop asking.

Thanks for using this resource.

Jerry Jones

Jerry lives on the East side of China with his wife and two children. His job and his life's passion are to equip global people. You can learn more about him and get access to other great resources for expats, repats and more at:

www.thecultureblend.com

Made in the USA
Columbia, SC
21 March 2025